LIBRARY

PEOPLES CHURCH LIBRARY
EAST LANSING, MICHIGAN

Encountering Myself

OTHER BOOKS BY HARRY JAMES CARGAS

Harry James Cargas in Conversation with Elie Wiesel
Religious Experience and Process Theology
Daniel Berrigan and Contemporary Protest Poetry
Death and Hope
English as a Second Language
The Continuous Flame: Teilhard in the Great Traditions
Graham Greene

Encountering Myself

CONTEMPORARY CHRISTIAN MEDITATIONS

Harry James Cargas

A CROSSROAD BOOK
THE SEABURY PRESS
NEW YORK

1977
The Seabury Press
815 Second Avenue
New York, N.Y. 10017

Copyright © 1977 by Harry James Cargas. All rights reserved. No part of this book may be reproduced, stored in a retrieval system, or transmitted, in any form or by any means, electronic, mechanical, photocopying, recording, or otherwise, without the written permission of The Seabury Press.

Printed in the United States of America

Library of Congress Cataloging in Publication Data

Cargas, Harry J   Encountering Myself.
"A Crossroad book."
1. Meditations.   I. Title
BV4832.2.C266   242   76-56519   ISBN 0-8164-0372-4

Contents

Foreword IX

PART 1
THE PERSONAL DIMENSION

1 A Watershed of History 2
2 Image and Likeness 4
3 Christ Died for *Me*? 6
4 Second Coming 8
5 The Hidden Me 10
6 I am Faust 12
7 My Truth 14
8 One Thing at a Time 16
9 On Being Busy 18
10 Goal 20

PART 2
LOVE AND DEATH

11 Love 24
12 On Being Loved 26
13 Love is Vulnerable 28
14 Unrequited Love 30
15 Love and Death 32
16 Worse than Death 34
17 No Such Thing as Half-Dead 36
18 Death Is Alone 38
19 A View From My Death Bed 40
20 Death as Prayer 42
21 Write Your Own Obituary 44
22 The Full Measure 46

PART 3
FAITH IS TRUST

23 Faith and History 50
24 The Christian as a Hindu 52
25 Religion as Expression 54
26 Betting on God 56

27	Mystical Body	58
28	In the Tone of Christ	60
29	Instant God	62
30	The Presence of God	64
31	Has Christianity Begun?	66
32	Prayer as Risk	68
33	Today's Martyrs	70

PART 4
THE WORLD AND I

34	Acts Are Meaningful	74
35	A Special Place	76
36	Holocaust	78
37	The Persecutors	80
38	Christians of Silence	82
39	Persons, Not Things	84
40	Subjects or Objects	86
41	Worry	88
42	Masculine/Feminine	90
43	Friendship	92
44	On the Shoulders of Giants	94

PART 5
ETERNAL QUESTIONS

45	Questions Without Answers	98
46	Time, the Great Ally	100
47	Tradition Is Not Convention	102
48	Suffering	104
49	Our Crosses	106
50	Lonely Is Not Alone	108
51	Saints	110
52	The Sanctity of Words	112
53	Freedom	114
54	Luxuries	116
55	On Being Perfect	118
56	Two Kinds of Knowledge	120
57	Children and History	122
58	Reincarnation	124
59	Theologians All	126

Foreword

Harry James Cargas is one of the few people in the world who seem to me to have any sense. I have read these meditations and I am very much moved by them, especially the ones on death and love.

The chapters on love are right. The albatross opens himself to vulnerability in courting the female. Love that finally consumes is based not on any "strength" but on the albatross act, the total vulnerability. I take these essays very personally. I know that now, as my life proceeds and my strength ebbs, I only regret those times when I failed in this openness to mercy and love, when I did not risk everything, when I held back some reserves of strength, just in case . . .

The pieces on death, too, are notable. As one approaches death, the near total destruction of all strength of body and perhaps of mind somehow tears away the last veils that separate one from a kind of direct contact with truth, beauty, love, mercy. One can experience people in a way similar to an extraordinary hearing of

Mozart and Bach—entering the heart directly with a kind of transparent, unguarded love. There is no longer any fear or need to hide anything from anyone. That is a great mercy and consolation rather than something to be greatly feared.

I find no facile, easy cliches and formulas in Cargas' writings. God love him for that. He has obviously gone through enough anguish to prevent his separating, as so many of us do, his fine mind from the heart's recognition of reality.

John Howard Griffin

PART 1
The Personal Dimension

For Nicki and Bud Thomas
with love

1
A Watershed of History

If I see myself as a watershed of history, I can more easily understand my own significance. The concept that Christ died for each person, each single individual, is lost on many of us. We can't imagine that we are worth such cosmic attention. We often seem to see ourselves as forgotten sand grains on the huge oceanic beach. And yet each of us is indeed the point in time wherein all history culminates and the entire future begins. Everything that has gone before finds its meaning in me. What a tremendous responsibility that entails. On a more personal level, I am carrying the blood of my parents, grandparents, ancestors, and beyond them. Do I take it forward or backward? Am I giving this meaning to their lives or that? Nikos Kazantzakis, the great Greek novelist, poet, playwright, and essayist, knew about this responsibility to his genealogical family when he wrote his autobiography, near the end of his life, as a "Report to Greco" (his long dead grandfather). Kazantzakis has given an account of what he had done with his life. Each of us could profit greatly from such a rendering—not only once in life but daily, hourly. And what of the future? Are we conscious of a responsibility to our children, be they physical or spiritual progeny? If I am the true start of the test of history, it is of ultimate importance that I live my life on the highest level possible. What "highest level" means for each of us will, of course, differ and must be determined by each of us for our individual selves. The meaning will be arrived at with careful reflection and great prayer. It will not be easy to find out that level, and we may find our "answers" changing from time to time—all of this hopefully indicative of some growth on our part. With it all, each can perhaps more fully realize that overwhelming aspect of a vocation as a human being: to be a watershed of history.

2
Image and Likeness

I am *made* in the image and likeness of God but whether or not I maintain that image effectively, whether I develop in it, depends on me. I reflect God most by participating in the ongoing Creation. One of the most significant descriptions of God is "Creator." That ought to be one of the important denotations of persons, too. Not "creator" in the restrictive sense of sculptor, composer, author, woodworker, and the like, but in an even more fulfilling and participatory way—creator on the fully human level. How creative are we in our approach to human relations? Are we creative in problem solving, homemaking, job delineations? If I am content to go along with the way it's always been done, to be led in all things, if I take the easy approach to existence, I'm lazy. I'm uncreative. I am in a very real way already dead. People are different from animals. People can make, can create, can participate in effecting the direction and speed of growth toward omega that the world will take. What a profound vocation each therefore has. And what a remarkable failure when we miss with our lives. Parents are called upon to be creative daily, hourly, with their children. Spouses who care do the same with each other. Such also is the ideal teacher-pupil relationship and that of neighbors and nations as well. So the woman or man who suppresses imagination only cripples. Political propaganda and all advertising are geared toward such mental paralyzing. Those of us who think only in cliches—the lazy way that is, through somebody else's words/ideas—do not respect ourselves enough to wish to work at development. Because, of course, the ultimate subject of creativeness, as well as the initial subject, is the self. If I sincerely work at continually recreating the self, I cannot help but recreate the universe. I am its center and when I shift, the entire world does. And, conscious of this, I can significantly help to renew the face of the earth.

3
Christ Died for Me?

How seriously do I believe that Christ died for me? For *me*. How has the consciousness of this revelation formed my life? Is the thought always before me as a guiding principle? Clearly it should be if I regard myself as a Christian. Of course, I claim to believe this, but if I really do, can it be said that the way I lead my daily life reflects this awareness? That Christ died for me gives me tremendous worth. I am, as it is, infinitely valuable; I have been redeemed by an infinite sacrifice. Do I see myself as someone of consequence? I should since, for me, God sent the only begotten Son. Well, if I am, in such a sense, the center of a universe, am I acting in a fit manner? We might be aware that petty behavior is *not* what is called for. Rather, action befitting one for whom Christ died. For example, should a person who so received the attentions from God the Creator be a gossip? Or a chronic complainer? Am I particularly quick and eager to blame others when the chance arises? Do I really believe in the dignity of my own life? Goethe wrote that good manners have their basis in heaven—Are my manners reflective of this? There is a tremendous responsibility put on me as one who has "benefitted" from the crucifixion. How have I accepted this? By cheating in little business deals? By admiring athletes who break the rules and don't get caught? By encouraging others to hedge on certain regulations? Do I use language befitting one for whom Christ died? Am I anxious to make snap judgments about other persons, often to their disadvantage? Do I, in fact, reflect enough on what it means that Jesus made me the great gift of himself? That has got to be a humbling thought when realized. Yet it is possible that most who call themselves followers of Christ fail to fully deal with this concept. If we did, most of us would change our lives radically. What does it really mean in my life? Christ died for *me*?

4
Second Coming

Perhaps the second coming of Christ has happened for each of us, but we don't know it; Christ is present to us and we do not recognize him. There is a long story by Henry James that may help illustrate this. He titled it "The Beast in the Jungle." It is about a man who confides in a woman, over the years, that something important is meant to happen to him in life and when it does, he will seize the event to live life to the fullest. Years pass and the event never appears to occur. The woman dies, and it is only then that he realizes that *she* was that event—her selfless love was what he should have seized upon in order to return it as fully as he could. However, in his self-centeredness he could not recognize the truth of their association. How true may that be of each of us in our relationship with Jesus? Are we in danger of passing through life virtually unaware that Christ is already present to us and in us? "Awareness" is, after all, an important aspect to Christian virtue. No Christian worthy of that title should plunge stupidly onward with all kinds of spiritual and psychological blinders on and miss the point of living. The "reappearance" of Christ is continually happening in me. But my ego-oriented person may be unable, unwilling to notice. Perhaps my *self* is so huge that I don't want to make room for another, even if that other is the Savior. None of us would admit to such a mentality, but perhaps we should examine ourselves concerning such a state nevertheless. The man in James's story was waiting for "his" beast to spring from the jungle and give new meaning to his life. Christ may be seen as our sacred beast who has already made his divine gesture to us, and it has, for too many, gone unremarked. To see a second coming as only a future occasion may be to look forward when we should be examining the present. It may be to look outward when we need to be searching inward. If, for the individual Christian, the second coming has happened—is happening—to miss it could be the monumental tragedy.

5
The Hidden Me

Sometimes I feel as if God has hidden me from myself and I'm trying to discover me. I know that the person I'm searching for is within. But that isn't enough knowledge. I'm there, all right, but what I perceive now is not the total, ordered self, but rather a fragmented and severely jumbled puzzle. I need to see more and I have to recognize a truer pattern. Sometimes I seem to come close. It's as if I were on the verge of the great spiritual discovery which is the purpose of my voyage, but just when I have thought the land of fullness was sighted, there turns out to be more oceans of emptiness. Perhaps there is my difficulty. Maybe the resolution is *in* the vast waters and I am failing to see that. However it may be, I am pained by my inability to find the real me, the "I" which gives total meaning to my existence. Possibly I am trying to navigate alone when I need one who is greater than I to be my guide. Will I trust Christ to help in this seeking of the self? Will I give Jesus free reign to do with me as he will and promise my faithfulness regardless of where the search leads? How much truth can I bear? Am I willing, indeed eager, to take what for the Christian is the ultimate risk, the absolute surrender to Christ? I know from several attempts that this is so very difficult. I've probably understood that the prize of self-knowledge is so great it is worth the sometimes terrifying journey. Yet what I embark on, each time I try again to sail the waters, is a trip guaranteed to result in a successful outcome. The end is guaranteed in the blood of Christ. Could there be a greater covenant? Is it possible that a more certain assurance could be offered? It is not. Then why do I fear to travel? Why am I weak with anxiety rather than eager with confidence? The contract that Jesus and I have, which promises me a fulfilled search if I will only undertake it with seriousness, is in fact binding to both parties. Can I accept his promise—and make my own to him?

6
I am Faust

The theme of Faust is one that has haunted Westerners for centuries. Basically it tells a story of a man who sells his soul to the devil. He promises to willingly accept hell for eternity in exchange for something he desires here on earth for as long as he lives. Part of the terrifying fascination of this theme is that many of us may feel that we could easily play the lead role in this tragedy. Is it true that I have my own price? Will I spiritually "sell out" if the reward is right? An examination of goals is very important here. What are the ends to which I am dedicated? Is the acquisition of material wealth my goal? What will I do to get it? Cheat? Lie? Steal? Fudge on my income tax? Do some "tricky" accounting work? The list of questions could be quite long. Or am I concerned with what I consider to be necessary sexual gratification with another person—let us say even though I or that other person (or both of us) are married to other people? What price will I be willing to pay for the "suspension of rules" in that case? Perhaps it is fame that attracts me. Will I *use* other people to achieve my end rather than *relate* to them? Am I more apt to give my attention to people who can "do me good" rather than to the "little people," to women and men and children who can't help me in my career, but who, perhaps, could be helped by me? Or little people who are simply a pleasure to be with—do I ignore them because there are no practical benefits in the relationships? In a certain way, such unvirtuous actions as these questions suggest imply a Faustian tendency in all of us. We at least toy with the notion of sacrificing everything in order to achieve certain aims. If the goal is less than spiritual perfection, the means will be considerably less than spiritually perfect. Reward in this lifetime is simply that. For what does it profit any of us to gain the whole world at the cost of our souls, our humanity?

7
My Truth

Just as we say that we must look at ourselves both as members of the entire world body and as individuals, so, too, I must seek universal truth as well as my own personal truth. These are not contradictory or exclusive truths, they are in harmony. Yet the part of the great truth which is my very own truth is unique to me. My task then is to search for that which is mine—which is me, really—find it, and then seize it, make it so conscious a part of my existence that it informs everything that I do. Another way of saying this is simply to realize that I am unique, to try to discover in what way I am unique, and then to develop this uniqueness in the service of the common good. I must caution myself that this has nothing to do with eccentricity, showing off, cultivating a difference for the sake of being different. Rather I must try to find out in what way I am different from all others who live, have ever lived, and who will live, and offer this difference to God in the important effort to try to complete the reality of humanity. As youngsters, we tried so hard to conform to what others did and were; we wished to be accepted as part of the crowd. We wanted, or seemed to want, the values, the ideas, the outer appearance (hair, clothing) similar to others. Advertisers and governments would love us to keep such an immature attitude: We would be much more manipulatable in this way. Hopefully, we are past that. But the growth of our spirit requires that we do other than just go along with the crowd, just live an unthoughtful life, just muddle on in time on a material, sensual, animal level only. The great adventure of my life is to find out who I am. This means finding my uniqueness, my truth, glorying in it and living it as heroically as I can. It may mean, actually, to live unheroically on a heroic level.

8
One Thing at a Time

There is a great need for those of us who live in frantic urban environments to learn the Zen teaching to do one thing at a time. Concentration is certainly a key concept in achieving certain goals, and this could be no less true where the spiritual life is the subject. In baseball, we are told that the hitters (pitchers, fielders) are most successful when they concentrate on the ball. In studying, performing music, loving, driving, cooking, the principle is exactly the same. The person who reads poetry while at the same time listening to music does justice to neither art. How much more true this notion is when applied to personal relationships and to prayer. The woman or man working toward perfection—a calling we all have by the very nature of our humanity—will work very hard to simplify life, to concentrate on one activity at a time. It would be silly to think that Saint John of the Cross achieved the level of mystical rapture he did if, while contemplating, he also mulled over chess problems in his mind. Nor is anyone truly interacting with another person if, at the same time, he or she is playing games, wondering "What can you do for me?" or in some other way manipulating that person. Again, we do not interact on a fully human level with our children, or with anyone else, if while talking with them we are thinking about what we'll wear tonight or the latest TV plot or how the business day went today. Probably most automobile accidents result because of a lack of concentration by the drivers *on the act of driving*. How many spiritual accidents or accidents in human relationships also result because of similar carelessness? Of course, total commitment of mind to particular acts and encounters is not easy. It is, in fact, very difficult and a process toward which we must work with great energy and discipline. But the calling to be fully human is not the easy way. We must be convinced the effort is worthy of us—and we must become worthy of the effort.

9
On Being Busy

There is a character in Chaucer's *Canterbury Tales* who tries to appear always engaged in meaningful activity. The author describes him as someone very busy, yet who seemed busier than he was. That is a condemning kind of judgment that may apply to many contemporary persons as well. Perhaps we all know the woman or man who is constantly active, working very hard, and achieving little else than a kind of unholy exhaustion. Rest, relaxation, time for reflection are absent from such people's lives. These more composed periods, so necessary for the refurbishing of the soul, are never allowed for—and this is to the serious detriment of an individual's spirit. It is apparent that many twentieth-century urban dwellers have the ability to do a lot of work, but others seem not to have the ability *not* to work. Rather than be still, than attempt some periods of adjustment to the harmony of the universe, than listen to God, than quietly extend their spiritual antennas in the direction of nature's wavelengths, these people choose to be busy. Card parties, bingo games, rummage sales, ball games, telephone committees, extended lunches, overinvolvement in our children's activities, and so much else can be excuses for not relaxing. Such busyness is frequently a cover-up by people who are afraid to think about what is really important to human development. If my serious interests revolve around the barber shop, the baseball score, the stock market tape, or the overall appearance of my car, I am clearly in a very shallow spiritual state. And this is dangerous, literally dangerous, to my growth as a full person. So often we generate less meaningful activity around our children or in connection with our church and rationalize what we do that way. Symbolic of this might be the parish rummage sale where women get together to gossip and to sell useless and broken items to the less fortunate and then feel good about their charitable endeavors.

10
Goal

A purposeless life is not a fully human life. Only an existence aimed toward a *significant* goal can approach the fully human experience. Perhaps right now is a good time to ask myself "Why am I alive?" This can be a terrible and frightening question. It can also be a very liberating one, however, and that is the sense in which we ought to ask it of ourselves. We are all alive and with certain energies. Are these energies coordinated and directed toward the ultimate meaning of the universe (we are called to nothing less), or is our attention focused on bridge parties, football, being popular, in fact gaining the world while losing our souls? Who will do the work of Christ if I don't? Who will lead me to wholeness if I don't? It is too easy to waste our time, our resources, our work. There are some persons who read a great amount, yet their scattershot approach to that activity keeps them from really *knowing*. There are others who read with a purpose. They select which newspaper articles, magazines, and books they wish to study in greater depth. They *take* reading material that's important to them to the doctor's office and do not leave their reading to chance, to whatever magazines happen to be in the doctor's waiting room. There is a principle of order, of goal orientation, operating here. A similar approach is taken toward life by the woman or man serious about self, about vocation, about God. Christ died for bridge players, too, but not for them *as bridge players*. The beer-drinking football addict may be redeemed, but not because he quaffs the nut brown ale and escapes into sport fantasy. Christ either has meaning in our lives or not. There's no middle ground, no "partial meaning." If he does, then the direction our lives take will show it. We will be goal-oriented Christians. The phrase, in fact, is redundant.

PART 2

Love and Death

*For Nancy and Ed Schapiro
and O'Ray Graber
gratefully*

11
Love

The major effect of love is that it brings us outside of ourselves. When I love, I choose a thou over me, over my own self interests. This is true in every case of mature love. And love has another value too, as the Christian realizes: It is my lifeline to Christ. In loving another I also confirm a relationship with Jesus that is meant to be fulfilling for one as a person. How sad for the person who cannot maintain this link. Christ himself *established* the link and gives us the ability to maintain it, but it is, of course, up to us to utilize this "power." One could be facile and suggest that this is a very easy task we are given to do as Christian human beings; we have not been urged to conquer the world or to master a vast body of erudite knowledge or to develop particular physical skills. "All" we are given to do is love. But such an observation is too simplistic. In one sense it is true; all we are told to do as Christians is love. But that all is a supreme all. It is everything in a spiritual way. Love is not easy. The great mystics of history, those tremendous lovers of God like John of the

Cross, Theresa of Avila, Meister Eckhart, Jakob Boehme, Martin Luther King, and others prove this from their experiences. Love is very difficult, it must be cultivated, worked on, developed, prayed over. It is a surrender of the self in the sense of risk. The lover says to the beloved, I give myself to you in a certain way in the confidence that you will not destroy me. Thus every act of Christian love has about it the elements of both risk and hope. To say "I love you" is at once to risk not being loved in return, while hoping for the desired reciprocity of feeling. Every act of love is a reflection of God's love for us. God too, in human terms, risks our refusal but hopes for our affirmative response. God's love, in some measure, is also therefore an act of trust. How much, then, do we trust in our relationships? The woman or man confident in Christ will repeatedly take chances on loving.

12
On Being Loved

While we frequently give some attention to the act of loving, we may be overlooking the more passive role of allowing ourselves to be loved. This is a very difficult, humble, yet important phase of our development as full persons. For one thing, it requires a certain disposition. We must allow ourselves to be open to others so that they may be open to us. Only through such relationships can real love take seed and grow. If we are closed to others, through fear or snobbery (which may well be fear in disguise), through ignorance or lack of trust, or for whatever reason, we may be destroying incipient love. (The same may be true on the international scene, in relations between nations, but that is another topic.) Perhaps implied in all of this is a large measure of self-respect. I might not be disposed toward "accepting" someone else's love if I do not love myself. The psychologically healthy person—and this means the spiritually healthy man, woman, child—is one who has a good image of self. Not an inflated or otherwise inaccurate image, but a balanced one. Humility is, as we know, the recognition of things as they actually are. Clearly this is what is involved in forming our self-images and consequently in preparing ourselves for both loving and being loved. We are told by contemporary psychiatrists that many persons are love starved. This is partly true because they are unloved and partly true because they cannot love. It is likely that many people do not love because those whom they know refuse to let that love "in." Not loving is crippling to the self. Not allowing the self to be loved is crippling to another self. Either way, no risk is taken, yet everything is lost. Spiritual, emotional progress can only be made through risk of love—active and passive. Which of us, when asked for bread, would respond by offering a stone? On the spiritual plane, unfortunately, the answer seems to be "many of us." It is as equally tragic to close ourselves off from the love of others as it is to refuse to love them. Why do we do it?

13
Love Is Vulnerable

When the male albatross courts the female, he makes obvious his intentions by raising one wing in such a manner that he makes himself vulnerable to attack. He is, in effect, saying I trust you. My purposes are honorable, and with this act of trust I prove it. There is a tremendous lesson for us in this act of faith in another creature. Are we ever willing to risk as much to prove our own love? Loving is a risk, and we are all engaged to some degree in a community of risk. The degree to which we immerse ourselves in this community may well be the measure by which we can realize our wholeness as persons. In loving we *choose* to make ourselves vulnerable; we say to another person that our relationship will not be based on fear. We will be honest with one another. You will learn things about me over which other people might laugh. I believe that you will not laugh. You will learn things about me over which other people might become angry or disappointed. I believe that you will not become so easily angry or disappointed. I bare my soul to you in a manner in which you can ravage it if you so choose, but I trust that you will not ravage but love instead. This is reflective of our relationship with God. We trust God in a supreme way. We constantly open ourselves to the Infinite if we are spiritually healthy, and we can be confident that we will not be demolished. On a person to person level, there is the countervalue of this, as well. We must be sensitive to others so that when they lift their wings to us we do not attack their weak spots. It is not easy to do so, but loving seeks not the easy route. Even when we feel that we have been misunderstood or been attacked, if we are sincere lovers, we will not attack in return. To love sometimes means to absorb pain. It should never mean to deliberately administer pain. And if we make this an integral part of our own personal attitudes, we will not limit ourselves to one person or one family but extend our love as widely as we can.

14
Unrequited Love

If it's not just the selfish, Hollywood type of pseudo-emotion, unrequited love is, nevertheless, *love* and that is all to the good. Christians claim to believe that love is a kind of energy that moves the world in a path toward union with God. If that is true, then all love is good and no love is wasted. No one who sincerely loves need be ashamed or disappointed because of that love. The Christian understands that by its very nature love is godful. (We have to keep reminding ourselves, however, that we are speaking of disinterested love, of that which desires good for the other person, for the recipient of that love. This may be rare in our lives: It may be that rare pearl of great price which scripture tells us about.) So any act of love is rooted in God, is supported by God, even contributes to the development of God in the sense that process theology speaks of such development. If I am a truly selfish person, I may think that I want something back for my love or I'll withdraw my affection. This is hardly a pure emotion; it is too much based on a scale, on a measurement. Love is not meant to be democratic in the sense that all love should be somehow "equalized" between participants. Selfless love is a giving that does not tabulate the degree of reciprocation. The honest lover simply gives and is even grateful for the opportunity to give. It is this kind of unpossessive charity that, the Christian knows, directs history. Political leaders have a tendency to speak of their country's acts as being judged by "Is this best for the national interest?" For the lover to have such an attitude would be a spiritual disaster. What's in it for me? That's how the thought translates into *personal* idiom. The man or woman who wishes to be recognized as a Christian cannot maintain such a false spiritual posture. Loving, with no terms attached, is what mature Christianity is about. We will not necessarily achieve a totally altruistic love, but we are urged to attempt it. When Christ asked us to be perfect, even as his Father is in heaven, he knew that was not possible. But to strive—that is fully human.

15
Love and Death

Love is the spiritual counterforce to bodily death. Death is negative, life destroying. Love is positive, life supporting, even life creating. Death is physical, love is not. Perhaps the most consistent manifestation we have of death in our daily living is in the form of loneliness. This sense of separateness, of total alone-ness is an experience of death. We are not lonely when we feel truly loved. It is common for sociologists and psychologists to talk about the lonely urbanite who lives and works in crowds. But we never hear of the lonely fiancee or the lonely person in a loving family. We also know of the spiritually oriented men and women who are always in the company of God who loves them. And it is the love of God that is our absolute protection against loneliness, that gives us our total victory over death. The woman or man confident of God's love cannot be lonely, will not fear death. This confidence is no doubt rare, and it may even wane a little occasionally in the hearts of those who have it. (Great saints, those as confident of God's love as human beings have been allowed to be, write of the dark nights of their souls.) But the point of value is not thus reduced. Love, in a very real meaning, is the *opposite* of death. When we perceive that love is life creating, we do not mean this in a biological sense: Animals procreate, but we do not suggest that they are capable of love in the way persons are. Rather, love is seen as a spiritual force, a radical energy, that rejuvenates that which might be almost inert, or possibly moves life in another direction. These experiences are very creative, very life giving, certainly very life sustaining. The person who loves, then, mirrors Christ and conquers death for self and others, because no act of love is isolated, even if it is very private. All love is a sharing with all of history, past, present, and future. All love is prolife and antideath. And we are not lonely in proportion to how much we love and are loved. Put in this context, we can easily conclude how terrible indifference is, not to mention hatred, in words and deeds.

16
Worse than Death

Is there anything worse than death? Are there certain things we would choose not to do, even if such a choice meant we would die? It might be an interesting exercise to list those general circumstances under which we might prefer death to life. We could learn much about ourselves by doing so. Does integrity rank higher than death in our values? What about honesty, love, friendship, and, of course, the traditional virtues? If we rank life as the most important good, as that which is most worth preserving *at all cost*, then we are saying something about ourselves, too. Is my own personal survival (which, in the scheme of history is only momentary) so important that I would, to choose exaggerated examples, be a Judas, participate in Watergate, cooperate with the extermination of Jews, murder an enemy, betray my nation, rather than die? How much are we really committed to living by principle? This is not an easy question, as is evident. For example, how important is a citizen's freedom to me? If the government tells me I may not worship God, am I willing to suf-

34

fer, to die, to insist on my right to be free? What if the government decrees that no male may have long hair? That, too, is an invasion of my area of personal freedom. Would I die for *that*? The one case obviously is of greater seriousness than the other. The point worth establishing here, however, is this: There are (or there are not) circumstances in life that are more intolerable than death. The cliched notion that something worth living for is worth dying for can be reexamined in the investigation of this question. (People have turned that thought around and insisted that something worth dying for is worth living for.) It is rather easy to look back at well-known figures and wonder how they chose betrayal (Benedict Arnold) over honor, or massacre (My Lai) over integrity, or life at any value over an honorable death. Most of us, of course, have small rather than heroic decisions to make regarding events in our lives. Yet the examples of Socrates and Christ are there for us, too. Why?

17
No Such Thing as Half-Dead

Actively placing ourselves in a religious tradition is not a part-time activity. We are either fully committed or we are not. It is also inaccurate to speak of someone as being half-dead. A person is either alive or not. In the same way, we cannot describe ourselves as somewhat religious or Christian in many ways. We either are or we are not. Our belief and coordinate actions resulting therefrom are a condition. As such, they are total or they are nothing. This is not to imply that we do not have problems or failings. Religion is not so simple a condition, of course. But it does mean that we are willing to struggle with the problems, struggle to overcome our failures, because we consciously want to—because we love God. And because we want to love people. Not abstract people, that great mass of humanity out there, but because we earnestly want to love Henry who has bad breath and Wilma who giggles a lot and Jonathan who talks a great deal about Jonathan and little Julie whose idea of conversation is relating the plot of the latest movie she has seen. Working hard in a religious tradition means working hard at loving, working hard at perfecting ourselves. It means knowing, too, that where we don't fully succeed, God will understand and cooperates in our attempts to do better. This confidence that we can have in God will assist us greatly in the absolute commitment that we make. Human beings are by nature gregarious, and religion is by definition a profoundly sharing experience. No Christian is ever alone. No Christian need be lonely because we can have the knowledge that Christ is fully with us (the question only being "Are we fully with Jesus?"), and the entire body of believing Christians is also one community sharing our burdens, joys, achievements, griefs, failures, successes.

18
Death Is Alone

Death is the meaning of life. It is the goal toward which all of our acts tend, consciously or unconsciously. Seen thus, death is a fulfillment in the ultimate sense. Death is the extreme point in self-creation. Every person is called upon to create the self to the fullest degree. It is at death that the process of my own self-creation will end. My purpose is to see that, whenever it is that death occurs, I am as fully prepared for it as I can be. This implies a worthiness to die. Do I deserve to die, in a certain sense? It is a holy death for which I ought to be preparing. Will it be? Perhaps the most difficult aspect of death for those of us in a materialistically oriented society is the truth that *death is alone*. It happens to me, by myself, naked before God. There will be no excuses for what I did or, perhaps more importantly, for what I failed to do. I'll not be able to point to everyone else who didn't act either and use that as an excuse. The call to Christianity is a call to the heroic life. Anything less is just that, less. With how much less are we going to be satisfied? Again, there will be no excuses. Not my classmates nor my clubmates will be able to intercede for me. Not my family nor my friends. Neither business associates nor drinking buddies. Not the bishop nor the commander of the American Legion Post. All of those people who think I am a good fellow have their opinions invalidated at the moment of my death. Only absolute truth is allowed then. Death is thus the real meaning of life. In that very important sense, each of us must be a philosopher, a kind of self-philosopher wherein what we learn that is meaningful we apply to our own self-creation. The French essayist Montaigne wrote that "to philosophize is to learn to die." Ancient Rome's Cicero said that "to study philosophy is nothing but to prepare one's self to die." The true philosopher, noted Socrates, "is always pursuing death and dying."

19
A View from My Death Bed

Lives have meanings. This is true of the individual life within itself and true of that same individual life within the human community. My life has an important significance *as my life*; it also has an important significance as an element in the great pattern of the universe. We do not always feel or acknowledge meanings in our lives. Some persons become apathetic, mentally ill, suicidal, because they fail to recognize a worthwhile uniqueness of their own contributions to the development of history. Psychiatrist Viktor Frankl has written that in the concentration camps that were part of the holocaust for millions of Jews in World War II, some perished who might otherwise have survived because they had not been able to find some meaning in their personal sufferings. This overwhelming subject cannot be discussed here, but out of his own horrible experiences in Auschwitz, Dr. Frankl has spoken eloquently of the individual's *will to meaning*. He suggests that one way we might come to some understanding or control over the direction of our lives is to project ourselves forward in time to our deathbeds. As I prepare to die momentarily and look back at my "achievements," are they what I would want them to have been? These "achievements" may have been in the sense of accomplishments (books written, children raised, bridges built, goals attained) or in the sense of experiences (true love of another person or persons, the sensing of truth, beauty, spiritual joy, meaning in suffering) or, hopefully, in both areas of accomplishments and experiences. It is not so difficult to do, to mentally jump ahead in time to the point of death—and this can be a very healthy exercise—the person who refuses to face the inevitability of death is the one who may well have the unhealthy attitude. And from the perspective of my own death point I may be able to realize the difference between a wasted life and a spiritually purposeful existence that could make an immense difference in the way I live from now on.

20
Death As Prayer

I wonder if it would be of value to see death as a possibility for prayer or under the aspect of prayer. Of course, in offering up my death, it may be so seen. But I mean more than this. Sain Cyprian says, "Let us embrace the day which assigns each of us to his dwelling, which on our being rescued from here, and released from the snares of the world, restores us to paradise and the kingdom of heaven. . . ." That's very positive, a very encountering kind of thing. Prayer has been called "response of God," and that fits comfortably with Cyprian's advice. Prayer is not so solemn that need always be seen as work. With that in mind, we may recall Dietrich Bonhoeffer's beautiful concept: "Death is the supreme festival on the road to freedom." Prayer, after all, is meant to bring us as close to being free as we can mortally become. Thus Bonhoeffer at least suggests the line I'm taking here, of death as prayer. Certainly we may conjecture that most deaths are no such thing. Nevertheless, death may be regarded as a prayer opportunity—possibly even *the* prayer opportunity. It is only at death that we may offer the summary of our lives to God and say here I am, fully yours, fully naked, fully willing to accept your judgment of my worth. God will know better than I who I am. Lagervkvist asks in one of his poems, "Lord over all heavens, all worlds, all fates,/what have you meant by me?" That's an overwhelming question, one we may ask ourselves daily, but only at my actual death may I ask it finally, fully. In a very absolute way, death is an experience I will face alone, with no crutches, no excuses; this will be *it*. But in another way, I'll be facing what all the dead before me have undergone, and it is not necessarily wrong to think that they may be continually offering their deaths along with mine in a momentous act of love to God on my behalf. It may be then that the concept of Mystical Body will have its fullest meaning for me personally.

21
Write Your Own Obituary

The obituary page of the newspaper is very fascinating to read. It is interesting to note what the persons who died are remembered for. At random, on any day that is, we can find notices of the deaths of a man famous for having been involved in a particular crime, or another who was a Salvation Army worker, a woman who was a wealthy socialite, an athlete, a person highly publicized for being an international bridge player, a nun, a teacher, a used-car dealer. And all of these are mentioned without judgment as to the quality of their work or their service to humanity. The question we might ask ourselves is this: How would my obituary look if it were published tomorrow? That might suggest a kind of negative ego trip, and it isn't meant in such a way. What is implied is this: What will my obituary be before God, before history? The newspapers rarely carry the death notices of "small" people, women and men and young people whose contribution to the welfare of all of us is that they were lovers in a fully human manner. We read how much money philanthropists gave to various charities, but that isn't the Christian way of judging. No condition in the next life can be purchased for cash in this one or measured on any scale of "amounts." But the idea of a spiritual obituary may be a valuable one. If I write my own, what would I highlight? Assuming, of course, my integrity. It is difficult to be objective, but . . . would I accurately say that I loved God in loving as many persons as I was capable? Perhaps I would have to face certain admissions of greed or lust or moral cowardice or sloth. Maybe I would have to examine more closely the motivations for my actions. Were they rooted in love and ethics or in convenience and selfishness? And, actually, how would *someone else* write *my* spiritual obituary? Does my true inner life show in a meaningful way? Could I *at least* characterize myself honestly as "one who tried"?

22
The Full Measure

How do we take failure? This is an extremely important measure of our Christianity. Do we know how to lose? Is our honor, our integrity, our love of humanity greater to us than the estimate other people have of us? If I am known as a good athlete, will I cheat or even just shade the rules a little to maintain that reputation? If student exaggerations have my name listed with the "all wise" teachers, am I able to say "I don't know" or do I give *some* answer so as not to appear ignorant? Or do I get very Darwinian in my business practices so as to maintain a number one ranking? So many of us, absorbed in that cliche known as the "rat race," get so dazzled by image maintaining that we duck asking ourselves essential questions: Would Christ do it this way? Is this what my Father wishes me to do? Christ is the great example here. He was willing to fail utterly in the eyes of humanity. Even his closest friends could not comprehend the meaning of his absolute failure on the cross. Yet how many of us, who are called to hang with him—to hang at least our beliefs, our actions, our true personal honor on that cross—are willing to risk the judgment of others? In being *unwilling* to risk the judgment of others, we are in fact risking the judgment of God. Of course, we probably wouldn't do so consciously. But if we do so without really thinking about it, we are surrendering our free will to mechanical, image-making motivations. We want to be at least as successful as the people in the ads or as certain neighbors or friends. Is my goal to please God or to enjoy the smug image of a self-divinized ego which is measured only in time against Madison Avenue standards rather than in eternity, against eternal criteria? The answer is easy; the practice very difficult.

PART 3

Faith Is Trust

*For Irma Grabowski
and Trudy and Charles Madden
in admiration*

23
Faith and History

Faith is an attitude we have toward history. In faith we acknowledge that all that has gone before is meaningful; not that we can now comprehend the full meaning of all of the events of the past, but an attitude that history is comprehensible—if only to an intelligence greater than the human. Faith is also an attitude toward the future. In this sense it is trust. We trust that life has, finally, a purpose, a goal, a meaning that is predicated on something beyond ourselves, beyond our sensualities, beyond our consciousness. This faith is very likely rooted in our unconscious. It is planted in our psyches before we are born. We inherit this attitude more profoundly than we inherit others, such as chauvinism, racism, or much more attractive "prejudices." It is probably, therefore, more difficult not be believe than to believe. An act of faith is probably a matter of "cooperating" with an unconscious bent we naturally have by virtue of our humanity (in the sense of our dependency). Resistance to this vital part of our total selves can be considered an unnatural act, a violence against our own very nature. And faith must be considered in the present as well. If it implies an acknowledgment of the meaning of the past and a trust that the ultimate pattern will be carried through the future, it also means something significant for the present moment. This seems to be bound up with action—a matter of showing the faith that is in us. This doesn't mean social work or letters to the editor or picketing to publicize injustices. It simply, and more importantly, means that faith is the basis for everything we do. If we picket injustices or visit the sick or work for world peace, we may do so on a secular level or on a supernatural level. Either way (in secularity or in faith) we will influence the course the mystical body or collective unconscious will take. It is clear that faith begets faith. Trust encourages trust. And a faith that is ever present is one with the meaning of history and the direction of the future.

24
The Christian as a Hindu

If I want to be a full Christian, I must be a Hindu and a Moslem and a Buddhist. Elie Wiesel believes that any person who is authentic assumes Jewishness. It is a truism that only in knowing other languages can we really understand our native language. The same can be said regarding the fullness of religious experience. Leon Bloy is correct when he says that the only tragedy is not to be a saint. What this means is that if we fail to be whole, we fail to be as human as possible, not that we ever achieve sanctity but that we keep on striving to achieve it. Christ knows we cannot be perfect as his Father is in heaven, yet he urged us to such perfection. Clearly he meant that we should always work toward the ideal. Define *saint* as we will, it is the only vocation. Why, when we ask youngsters what they want to be when they grow up, are we satisfied with answers like firemen, nurse, pilot, scientist, doctor, teacher, actress? Why don't we look more for a reply that will say "I want to be a whole person." Or even "I want to be happy" which is a synonymous saying. Jung writes that every man must develop the feminine side of hs psyche, every woman her masculine side. This will lead each to a more whole existence—the deep recognition of the *anima* and the *animus*. He suggests that Catholics have subconsciously recognized this need in the respect they pay to Mary: There was a necessity to include the feminine principle in the otherwise essentially masculine-oriented Christian tradition. So the ecumenical impulse is a body-wide movement toward unity, toward a wholeness which is admirable. And the more Jewish and Suti and Confucianist I become, the more Christian I can become.

25
Religion as Expression

Religion cannot remain on the level of idea alone. Religion must be an expression. It must be an incarnation in the real world of an ideal that is of supreme import to the individual of belief. Religion not only has to be worth living *for*, it has to be worth *living*. Faith on a theoretical level is a fossilized faith if it remains only on that level. We've all heard of the Catholic who never goes to church, never can really be identified as a Catholic from his actions but who, with a few too many whiskeys down his gullet, is willing, indeed anxious, to fight anyone who insults the pope. For too many of us, that's the level that our action based on faith takes. It's more than silly—it's damning. Too often religion *is* a joke. Why is it that in so many cultures the only people who are identified with spiritual beliefs are women, children, and old persons? The reason is because each of these groups is held in contempt by those out in the "real world!" And it is well known by them that religion has nothing to do with the real world. Reality has to do with business, with war, with politics, with agriculture, with industry. Imagine if religion somehow intruded its meaningless self into those areas! Well, for the true believers, we must not only imagine it, we must practice it. Business, war, politics, agriculture, industry, and all of the rest of the world's activities are too often conducted without a religious basis, without attention to the moral aspects of their doings. The historic tragedy resulting from this is on the tremendous scale of all humanity. Silent religion, religion which really has no effect on positive, outward living, is on the verge of the scandalous. No Christian is called to be a silent Christian. Witness need not take the form of crucifixion; it need not, in fact ought not, be obnoxious or offensive to others in most cases. But witness ought to *be*, ought to exist in our lives, or, in fact, we are not alive—not as self-expressive Christians or Jews or Moslems or Hindus or Jains or Buddhists, or . . .

26
Betting on God

It has been suggested that the clever person will pay homage to God because, if God exists, that person will be on the right wavelength; if God does not exist, the worshipper will not have lost anything that wouldn't have been lost anyway. Viewing faith as a good bet is both cynical and destructive to real spiritual growth. Perhaps more of us approach our religion that way than would care to admit—even to our selves. This, in fact, is a despicable attitude toward God, toward history, toward other humans, even toward our own personhoods. Faith is not a bet just as religion is not a game. We are not being asked something so silly as to wager our souls on a particular number of a celestial roulette wheel in order that we may be inordinately rewarded if that tumbling ball of grace plops in the correct slot. Rather we are asked to totally commit our spiritual selves, which means our complete selves, to a kind of harmony with the universe. This doesn't depend on luck. Salvation, however it is defined, has absolutely nothing to do with chance or good fortune. It depends on what it is we do, who it is we are. I do not have infused knowledge. I have a spiritual dimension, a spiritual learning, by the very nature of my humanity. I will either develop it or I will not. If I fail to do so, I jeopardize my relation with the world, with nature, with God. If I work at it, spiritual growth is a necessary, not a chance, result. Being alert to God, to the meaning of history in my life, requires constant vigilance. As in the scriptural story, we do not know when the bridegroom will come. But our faith informs us that indeed there is a bridegroom and indeed he is coming for us. He is continually coming for us. Our task, in the various ways possible to each of us, and they are many, is to be open to this coming, to continually prepare the way for the lord. Not out of gambling with the odds: if he comes I'll be ready, if there's no bridegroom I haven't lost anything anyhow. The God we are cooperating with is not a stupid God who will fall for something like that. We ought not be so stupid as to try it.

27
Mystical Body

The concept of the Mystical Body ought to be very real and personal to every Christian. It is an ancient idea that has been supported by contemporary thought in quite magnificent ways. Those in the Mystical Body of Christ share in the works and thoughts of all other members of that Body in some special way. Carl Gustav Jung taught that we all share in a collective unconscious, indicating that we are thus born with certain predispositions, attitudes, and that we are not born with minds that are simply *tabulae rasae*. Teilhard de Chardin described it somewhat differently in his presentation of the noosphere —that membrane of consciousness that covers the universe and in which we all partake. This means, in part, that not only am I influenced by the thoughts of Plato and Saint Theresa and the actions of Alexander the Great and Babe Ruth, but also by the thoughts and acts of average Joe Greek and Millie of the Middle Ages. There is a psychic continuity operating in the world that affects each of us. The idea of the Mystical Body of Christians has something to do with affirmative affecting which can be of great inspiration of each person aware of it. Furthermore, it makes understandable the nature of the obligations of each person to the rest of the world, past, present, and future. If I am part of the great continuity, then I must carry forward the flame of love handed to me. I must give the past as full a meaning in my life as possible. In addition, I must live as fully a whole life as possible so that what I leave the flame I hand on to many other hands will be as warm with the passion of Christ as I can make it. My obligation of integrity is tremendous. In love I am to help fulfill all that has gone before and assist in continuing in the proper direction all that is to come. Only committed persons, striving, striving with effort, can do the task properly.

28
In the Tone of Christ

To be a Christian means to strive to live as fully as possible in the atmosphere of Christ. This has to do with being a spiritual framework with Jesus; it has to do with lifestyle, with the tone of one's life. Christians are called to the spirit, the genius of Christ. But when we speak of style, tone, attitude, "temperature" if we may, this excludes any general notion of the occasional. Style and tone and attitude imply saturation, immersion. We must co-create in ourselves a presence that guides us in all our acts. Not only do we not murder because we love Christ, but we take our driver's turn at four way stops for the same reason. Not only do we not cheat our customers or our employers (or -ees) but neither do we cheat in games or cheer when we note an athlete getting away with something the referee couldn't see. Yet these are negatives. The person enveloped (but not sealed off!) in the atmosphere of Christ loves, transmits love, generates love. This is not easily achieved. Nor will it be as totally achieved as we might like. Nevertheless, each of us can come much closer to this ideal than we have up until now. We need to become conscious of the personal obstacles we each face to living in this tone of Christ. Perhaps I am less successful as a Christian in my attitude toward the world when I first arise in the morn or driving home from work or when with certain persons. Living in the aura of love doesn't *just happen* for most of us. When we see people we admire living in the genius of Christ, we may be beguiled into thinking it was easy for them. Undoubtedly this is not so. Undoubtedly it took tremendous effort to learn to cooperate with whatever grace it takes to realize this state of existence. Is the effort worth it? What's the meaning of life?

29
Instant God

The age of speed has unfortunately intruded on the spiritual world. People now seek, even demand, instant God, instant relevation. They fly from life and reality into what they regard as mystical experiences via drugs. They went to become Saint Theresas and Jakob Boehmes right now, eliminating the years of preparation, the *work* necessary to lay the foundation. It's almost as if they were trying to trick God into relating with them instead of themselves laboring to relate themselves to God. They attempt to build a very ornamental roof for a structure that has no foundation. True spirituality isn't an escape *from* something; it is a heroic leap *into*. Really heroic. Drug mystics cheapen the nature of mystical heroism. Instant heroism is no heroism at all; it is the very negation of struggle that is the foundation of heroic endeavor. Furthermore, the question becomes what happens *after* a mystical experience! The person who has cultivated a habit of mind, of prayer, of contemplation, will have her or his entire life flavored by a certain taste of the eternal, whereas the person who has had a quick Jesus-jag will just as quickly go on to something else as soon as that drug-induced spiritual thrill is finished. This makes a mockery of spiritual heroism wherein the faithful laborer shares not only joys but obstacles with God. But the hurdles are overcome with struggle in time (not with instant "victory") and a goal is reached. Furthermore, the true communal hero frequently comes back from the journey into mysticism and overcomes further obstacles to return to the rest of us and to share the new found bliss with us. This can be done only in time, a long time; there are no short cuts to spiritual perfection. There are no pills available that will enable me to play the violin masterfully in half an hour. The mere suggestion of that ridicules authenticity—the years of effort to purify the skill. The same is even more truer of the development of the interior life.

30
The Presence of God

Many of us would say that God knows all and sees all. Yet few of us act consistently with this *apparent* belief. If we did, how could we act in the manner we do, how can we contrive to dwell on the thoughts that we do? The holy men and women urge us to strive to live in the presence of God, to be conscious of God being fully with us every moment. Brother Lawrence, a seventeenth-century advocate of such practice and a simple, unsophisticated person as the world judges, lived his life in the presence of God for half a century. This humble man has said that it is not difficult to acquire the habit, that it does not take particularly long. The initial effort requires a great spiritual struggle— hard work that is—but soon this habit of mind can be cultivated, developed. Then God takes over. It is as if God has seen that we are sincere in our efforts to live continually in the divine presence, and so when we have the human tendency to lapse, God assists us. But God does not initiate the attitude in us. We are allowed our freedom here, as in all other things. But when we choose the spiritual path of trying to experience God's divine presence in us at all times, ceaselessly, then we will receive the assistance that we need. We can imagine the tremendous, the significant effect such an ongoing experience will have on our lives. If I am a political figure, all of my votes and decisions would be based on moral considerations. As a teacher, my work for the students would be my work for God—no more skimping on class preparations or short-tempered responses to those who don't catch on as quickly as I would wish. Again, our imaginations can help us to project the effects living in the divine presence might have on us as spouses, drivers, neighbors, members of a racial or economic group, citizens—the list is as long as each of us wishes to make it. Asking God's help to be with God and working toward this end can lead to "ordinary" life lived on a heroic level.

31
Has Christianity Begun?

When asked if he didn't believe that Christianity were a failure, G. K. Chesterton said that we couldn't make that judgment since Christianity really hadn't been practiced yet. George Bernard Shaw suggested essentially the same idea. More recently, I interviewed German Nobel-winning novelist Heinrich Boll, and I talked to him, a Catholic, about the religious situation in his country. He responded this way: "You know I sometimes think that Christianity didn't start yet. Up to now we've had churches and confessions and hierarchies and fighting and controversy. Maybe Christianity is to start now, in a different way—not always organized, not always looked after by authorities." Perhaps it would be in order for each of us to sincerely ask the state of Christianity in our own souls. How developed is it, in those of us who publicly claim to be members of this particular faith? Those who label themselves Christians are not necessarily such. Europe has long been designated a Christian continent, but *at least* the holocaust of the Jews made that a lie. And many will remember in this nation the spectre of "Christian" white men and women slandering Negroes *because they were black*. Some of these pariahs were even priests and ministers, official Christians in the eyes of the world. But, of course, it isn't the world that will ultimately decide the validity of such claims. I can too easily fool others. One of the great spiritual problems I face, in fact, is the ease with which I can fool myself. We have dramatically seen self-deception on national and international scales; we have seen it on the individual scale—in others—as well. Now how about the more personal level of ourselves? How much of a Jekyl-Hyde spiritual existence do we live? The difficulty is serious and it is real. One person with integrity, even living the most private life, affects the entire behavior of the universe. That is God's promise, and it is among modern psychology's great lessons. But the converse is also true. So with each of us empowered with this awesome ability, will we dare be less than as fully Christian as we can?

32
Prayer as Risk

To pray is to risk. Every act carries with it the possibility of failure. Nevertheless this realization ought not to keep us from *doing*. Rather it should increase our attention, our application, to what we are doing. This is of extreme importance in communicating with God. We need to be conscious of the manner and the content of our prayer. The manner is the "how." Is our prayer as sloppy as much of the rest of our life is? That's worth knowing. Do we really not care very much about ourselves or about God. If that is true, it will show up in how we pray. In prayer we are able, in a way, to demand the attention of the master of the universe. The process is, as it were, irresistable by God. So what do we do with this "ultimate spiritual weapon"? Am I disciplined enough to give my total self to this communication? Do I give God at least as much respect as I would if I were conversing with a football hero, a leading politician, a telephone caller? Or is this only a halfhearted ritual I engage in occasionally for form's sake, out of habit? Do I do it out of the merest routine in the same way that I, from time to time, brush my teeth, exercise, talk with the children about *their* ideas, which really don't interest me that much. The second element of risk in prayer, along with the manner or "how," is the content or "what." We can learn immensely about ourselves if we think about the kind of prayer we engage in. Is it usually on a gimme basis? Or do we bargain with God: I'll do this if you'll do that for me? What of the prayer of pure praise, of gratitude, and particularly the prayer of silence? In silence we come closest to the definition of prayer which is understood as listening to God. Silence before God is trust in God. To cultivate such an attitude may be like trying to escape an advertizing mentality, whereby we try to convince God that we are good products for investment. Prayer is a risk worth taking—and taking seriously.

33
Today's Martyrs

It has been an important part of Christian tradition that those who were martyred in Christ contributed greatly to the growth of the Church. Developments in contemporary psychology show this to be a very reasonable belief. Whether we speak in terms of Mystical Body or collective unconscious (Jung) or the noosphere (Teilhard de Chardin), we are saying that nothing that anyone does is lost on future generations. Every act and thought (good or bad) has its effect. The more significant the action or the thought, the more influential it will be. And since Christ told us that no one has greater love for a friend than the person who lays down his or her own life for that friend, we may understand more fully the value of a martyr's gift. What we may conclude about martyrs and others persecuted for Christ is that they were good women and men seen as bad people, as threats to some group's ideas of established order. We look back on history now and ask why it is that the citizens of "those times" couldn't see how wrong they were in persecuting Saint Peter, Thomas

More, Jon Huss . . . The list if very long. More appropriately, we might *ask ourselves* who are they among us who are being mocked, reviled, spat upon today. Who are today's martyred, today's sufferers for Christ who are the seeds of the future Church? Are they the Christian war resisters who refuse to participate in the killing of Christs—seeing Jesus in all people—though ordered to do so by their governments? What of the poor who keep getting legislated against by local officials and taken advantage of by realtors, bankers, grocery chains. . . . Again, the list is long. Where are the suffering Christs to be found today? We might look in our prisons for one answer. Another place is in juvenile institutions where our young are put in solitary confinement, are sexually abused, are tranquilized until their brains are damaged or they become addicted. Perhaps the most important question we might ask ourselves is "Am I one of Christ's persecuted?" The follow-up to that might be "Why not?" If I take my Christianity seriously . . .

PART 4
THE WORLD AND I

*For Alicia Remus
and Alex Kassel
in hope*

34
Acts Are Meaningful

Our acts reveal the meaning of our lives. Were we to study our deeds closely, we could learn a great deal about who we are, what our values are. So simple a routine as television watching may be used as one measure. For example: How *much* do I watch? Do I select the programs, or have I become their victim? (Do I watch specifically chosen shows or merely certain times?) Does "nothing" interfere with my favorite adventures, comedies, or football games? Are mealtimes TV times at our house, stultifying family communication? Another battery of questions could be applied to our work (just enough to get by, hatred of colleagues, etc.?) and to our interests. What do we *really* care about and therefore participate in? Is it true to say that I am very active in my children's school activities if all I take part in is the card party or stag barbecue? Have I done any more than feel sorry for the earthquake victims in Turkey or the neighbors on the next block whose house burned? Am I active in a practical way in politics or some other productive area, or do I merely curse the politicians and use that as an expression of the extent of my involvement? We are all called to be Gandhis, Martin Luther Kings, Schweitzers, Thomas Dooleys, to use these contemporaries as symbols. Of course, each of them had shortcomings as persons. To that we can say, "So have I." But each also had tremendous talents and strengths which he developed. Can each of us say to that, "So have I?" If God really counts in our lives, our acts will indicate that truth. An isolated or occasional action is not meant here. The thrust of all of the deeds of our lives as lived right now in this world is what this idea signifies. Excuses help nobody, particularly the individual using them. A mere handout for charity is not going to buy our way into spiritual communion which is, in the last view, what each of us is called by vocation of our humanity to do. Emphasis on *do*.

35
A Special Place

Meditation, contemplation, self-recollection, creation: In some ways these are all aspects of each other. They sometimes mirror, sometimes reenforce one another. The person who cannot engage in activities such as these does so at great risk to psychic wholeness. (Two words in the previous sentence are crucial: *engage* and *activities*. These imply commitment. Not only a willingness to work but an ability to do so. *Ability* does not mean, necessarily, some special skill, rather the time, place, and desire to do so.) To engage our spiritual selves on a significant level, we might profit immensely from having a cultivated environment where our meditation, contemplation, self-recollection, and/or creation can best be developed. Of course, each of these acts can be performed anywhere. But for most women and men, a special place, apart from the place of our everyday work, is very helpful to allowing freedom, to developing a mood—particularly quiet—to feeling a psychic distance between the now and both the before and the after. Some people find stopping by church during the day spiritually productive. They are relatively alone; there is no phone, no noise, no child or boss or employer demanding attention. Others find a corner of the yard, a walk in the neighborhood, a "break" in the den as extremely useful. Mood is very important and the environment is very important in helping to set the mood. This seems too simple to emphasize, yet so few of us, particularly those who live in the city, really can call a place our very own—a little retreat from the world where we can get ourselves together or even do the opposite, let ourselves go, relax from the daily tensions which are so counter productive to our spiritual well-being. Nobody expects a novelist to write in Grand Central Station or a homemaker to meditate in the kitchen just as the children return from school. We each need that special place.

36
Holocaust

As contemporary Christians, the holocaust must be regarded by us as one of the central tragedies of our heritage. The slaughter of six million Jews happened too easily. Christianity had nineteen centuries to take root; to grow into the tree of love that the tree of Christ's cross committed us to. Instead of love, deep human regard raised to a supernatural level through Christ's intercession, we could only come up with ovens for women, men, girls, boys. Afterward we have even raised the question "Why didn't the victims resist?" As if, somehow, the blame is to be put on those who were killed. That's only a trick to keep ourselves from considering the true meaning of Christ in the many so-called Christian nations. Germany saw themselves as followers of Jesus. In fact, it practically became a religious obligation for some to lead in the persecution of the Jews. The French, the Polish, the Hungarians—so many more—cooperated so readily or acted so indifferently to the machine gunning and gassing and torture that went on that we must—we must—wonder where was Christian morality? Charity, even minimal love, was absent. True faith was apparently almost nonexistent. And hope? Hope may have been dashed forever in the hearts of some because who can have hope in the promises of a Redeemer after Auschwitz? Perhaps neither Christians nor Jews can. My individual task has to be that of rebuilder. It is my vocation to become as much a person of faith and charity as I am able so that hope may once again abound in Christians. Maybe if this can take root in me, it can blossom in others. I have been diminished in a theological way six million times. The holocaust must never be allowed to happen again. And yet . . .

37
The Persecutors

People who are given to stereotyping other people will probably conclude, in about a quarter of a century, that the lowest human being in the world is a white, male, North American Christian. It would be wrong to stereotype in this way, but the categories are worth considering. Each of them is a category of persecution. And most of us belong to more than one of these groups. The white is seen as a persecutor by black men and women and children in this country, in Africa, and in Asia, where people with yellow skin have been made to feel inferior precisely because of the color of their skin. Males are also considered persecutors, slave masters, by a large segment of the world. North Americans, primarily those living in the United States, are regarded as the enemy by a significant percentage of the earth's population. One has only to read the popular fiction and poetry of South America to see the attitudes of those people toward certain United States political and economic policies. The same is true of much of Southeast Asia, some of the Arab world, Russia, China.

We are not thinking of the merits of the arguments raised by these peoples, we are simply observing certain historical facts. Most disappointing of all is the way the Christian is regarded in many pockets of society. Some Jews have a great distrust of us, based on a history of persecutions in which the holocaust was the most recent and overwhelming example. Asians see the Christian religion bound up with capitalism and/or democracy as well as with a missionary zeal which at times appeared dedicated to obliterating many traces of local culture. Africans, too, for years, had been told by Christians—ministers, nuns, politicians, military figures, and businessmen—that they, the Africans, had no indigenous culture. It is proper for those of us who are white, male, North American, and/or Christian to reflect on just what those categories mean in our lives.

38
Christians of Silence

History contains the stories of many Christians that were forced into silence to maintain their beliefs because of persecutions. In Japan, for example, Christianity went underground for several centuries because it was identified with political betrayal by the official government of that nation. Under such conditions, silence may be looked on as heroic and virtuous. But there is another side—a dark side—to the silence of Christians. There are circumstances when silence is sinful, is cowardice, is not only the easy way out but it is an absolute betrayal of Christian, and therefore human, values. In the face of racism, say, in the United States, silence among alleged Christians is abominable. The historical fact of the holocaust, which was different from a long series of persecutions of Jews by Christians perhaps only in degree, proved a test that many of us failed. Some who called themselves Christians actively destroyed Jews. It may be that hell was created for the likes of these killers. But what of the many silent (and therefore cooperative) "Christians" who knew of those atrocities and were unmoved by the mounting tragedy? And how visible are we today, *as Christians,* regarding such problems as starvation in Bangladesh or racism in Rhodesia or gross public immorality on the part of entertainers or illegel and immoral practices by our local realtors or when our neighbors tell jokes at the expense of ethnic or minority persons? In large things or in small, the Christian is called to witness. In a true sense, there can be no such man or woman who claims to be a Christian who doesn't want to be involved. A full definition of the term *Christian* implies involvement, discipleship, apostleship. A Saint Paul who did not wish to be involved is unthinkable. The same is true of Luther, Hus, Newman, Schweitzer, Martin Luther King, Mother Theresa. Even those of us who "stand up to be counted" on one or two issues too frequently remain contemptibly silent on others. As such, we are probably part-time Christians. That's a full-time tragedy.

39
Persons, Not Things

Sometimes we treat people as things. Then when we do, we can be conscience free in manipulating them. The whole business of advertising is based on that attitude. To take an extreme example, consider the encouragement we receive to smoke cigarettes. We know absolutely that they are harmful to health, yet some of us attempt to convince others of us to continue to purchase them *because it will be profitable* to some of us. And yet, when we consider the responsibility each of us has for all other human beings, the realization of such manipulation is horrifying. The question put to Jesus, "Lord, who is my brother?" elicited the story of the good Samaritan—the example of a non-manipulator. But in that tale there appear several characters that walked past the suffering man. They were able to do so because they did not regard his humanity—they saw him only as an inconvenience, a thing. We do the same with our own children when we manipulate them, when we practically try to trick them into going to the colleges we went to or into the careers we wish we had chosen, etc. We even *train* our youngsters to do the same when we encourage them to sell their Girl Scout cookies to the neighbors who "wouldn't turn you down" or when we allow our children to sell their toys to their companions who, momentarily at least, become more consumers than friends. On an international scale, if we treat people like things, we can break them. It would be difficult to urge soldiers to kill *fathers* and *husbands* and *brothers* from other countries. But when they are, instead, identified as communists or capitalists or Vietnamese or Americans instead of as humans, the act of destroying becomes much easier. On a lesser scale, we do the same when we gossip about a neighbor or co-worker; we are *killing* that person's reputation. It even seems that in our mad scramble for recognized success we abuse *ourselves* as things. Christ died for persons, not for things.

40
Subjects or Objects

Contemporary psychiatric exploration is proving some very important fundamental aspects of humanity that have great significance regarding the religious orientation of humanity. While early analysis emphasized how men and women are "driven" by sexual impulse or a will to power, more modern work is showing that those whose id is directing their lives are less than fully mature persons. Rather it is the woman or man who assumes responsibility for the direction the individual life is taking who may be regarded as most fully human. We may speak here, perhaps, of secular and spiritual meanings in life. (These terms are used in a quite specialized sense here.) The man or woman "satisfied" with the secular explanation of life might too easily be content with the concept of drives, of outside, unmanageable forces exerting such influence on us that we can do little of import to influence our own actions and desires. However, the person who sees a deeper, spirit meaning in the world and of the world cannot accept such a limited rationale for existence. Rather that person realizes in some fuller way her or his own dimension in the universe; her or his own responsibility to God, to humanity, to history, and to the future. Above all, perhaps, that person understands the responsibility of the individual to the present. Certainly we do not have to be conscious of the obligations to the past and to the future if we are working to live authentic lives in the now. Nor should the emphasis be on "working" as much as on creating, as cooperating with the continual creation process that is taking place in time—and particularly, for us, in *this* time. The assumption of responsibility is a serious one. But the very fact of humanly conscious existence is by definition a serious matter. We can slough it off: We often do and in fact are urged to do so by advertisers who constantly attempt to benumb us as consumers, as objects. Or we can be subjects, responsibly functioning subjects.

41
Worry

We ought not to feel guilty when we worry. It's Middle Ages' theology that says that to worry is to show lack of trust in God. It seems that with universal conditions being what they currently are, to worry is a virtue. Of course, this may be seen as an exaggeration, yet it does merit consideration. For worry is an extreme form of concern, and concern is good. The person who doesn't care, who can't be bothered, who fears involvement, who hasn't the time (which is otherwise spent at cards, Tupperware parties, and the like) is lukewarm at best—worthy of being rejected by the faithful *workers* at reckoning time. The worrier, at least, implies that there is something important enough to get uptight about! No one suggests that pathological worrying ought to be praised or cultivated. Rather, perspective is called for. But to become Pontius Pilates, to wash our hands of the world and not care what is happening in it, is to err seriously. In the Middle Ages, there was room for the spiritual counselor to tell us to leave all to God. Often, that guidance was being given to a monk or cloistered nun for whom that might quite properly have been a learned principle. But life is intensified. We now have drugs, Communism, automobiles, hydrogen bombs, violent revolutionary groups, alcohol, the CIA, nationalist terrorists, capitalists, the IRA, the NKVD, kidnappers, thrill seekers, handguns, motorcycle gangs; the list is terrifyingly long. So if life is intensified, concern will have to be intensified as well—and that is sometimes called "worry." But we need not necessarily feel guilty because of such mental involvement. Whether as citizens, as parents, as consumers, as spiritual people, as peacemakers, as providers, as seekers of truth, in whichever of these areas we may pass the bridge between concern and worry, we need not be automatically ashamed. We may need to work on control but not on negation of the feeling that something is getting out of control, something that is serious and worthy of attention. It really is possible that more people *ought* to worry.

42
Masculine/Feminine

"Big boys don't cry" is a terribly crippling concept. This volcano-capping idea is symbolic of what many persons feel is a separation between how men act from how women do. Such people have no notion of what wholeness is in a human personality. The reason is because they confuse male with masculine and female with feminine. Male and female are terms having to do with the physical makeup of human beings; masculine and feminine belong to a psychological realm. Because someone is born male does not mean that he should only develop masculine traits or only participate in so-called masculine sports or jobs. Women, too, have suffered because they, too, have been limited. Girls rarely played basketball, rarely grew into jobs such as business executives or doctors. Yet the terms masculine and feminine are not meant to imprison, rather they are liberating concepts. We ought to know when we are too one-sided. If, as a man, I am harsh, unforgiving, unflecting, otherworldly to the point of ignoring this earth, then I need to give serious attention to another part of my personal development. And a woman who is overly sentimental, coquettish, fearful of contact with the man's world is also only a small fraction of the whole person she can become. Jungian psychology reminds a man that he must develop his feminine side of his person and that a woman must develop her masculine side. This kind of integration will help lead to wholeness. Is the religious person committed to anything less than personal wholeness? To a growth that is a harmonious blend of whatever is best in the personal aspects of the universe? Too often we are afraid to take a chance to help ourselves psychologically, humanly. But the failure to do so leads in a direction opposite to which we ought to be traveling.

43
Friendship

A true friend takes you for who you are rather than for who you pretend to be. There is great security in that kind of a friend. There can be a level of trust there that seems necessary to growth in human relationships. And friendship on this very basic level mirrors our relationship with God. Certainly Christ knows us, even better than we know ourselves. He sees the core without the accrued camouflage, without the layers of masks we have adopted to keep the real us from appearing. Christ sees us so intimately and continues to love us so deeply that we should learn a great deal about ourselves from this. Each of us feels inadequate, on some level, to the task of being fully human and all that that implies. Christ knows our inadequacies, yet he loves us, even trusts us, to be ourselves. God trusts us so much that we were made free. We are created to develop along the path each of us chooses for our lives. No one else has given us that kind of liberty. The reason is, of course, that no one else loves us as fully as God does. As friends, how do we reciprocate? Am I essentially a friend who takes but one who seldom gives? I need to think about that question with some seriousness. God's love for us ought never to be one-sided. Clearly our love for Christ will never match his for us; nevertheless we must always be cultivating our love, nurturing it so it will grow toward fulfillment, even though never achieving it in this life. The various friendships that we have contain trust, love, respect, and time. We cannot have deep relationships without these elements. The same is true in the relationship that these worldly affiliations mirror—our personal interaction with Jesus Christ. The friendship that is always there, is always reliable, and one on which we can base our personal security. How fortunate we are.

44
On the Shoulders of Giants

Others have expressed the same sentiment, but perhaps Isaac Newton said it as well as any: "If I have seen further, it is by standing on the shoulders of giants." There is an admirable humility in such a remark, in the fullest sense of the concept of humility. First, Newton recognizes before the world that his could not have been a solo performance, that the way for any success he might have had was long prepared by countless others. Second, and this is equally important in the meaning of humility (in seeing things as they truly are) Newton is not afraid to admit that he has indeed seen further. To deny this would suggest a false humility, an inability or unwillingness to view the actual situation. Also implied in this sentence is the acknowledgment of a process; next will come men and women, few but worthy, who will stand on Newton's shoulders and contribute what they have to carry humanity ever onward toward its goal. Currently, in about two weeks, a good student in our schools can "learn" all of the physics Newton absorbed. But that does not make the student a giant, and it certainly does not diminish Newton's achievements or historical importance. One final implication to point to here is that Newton was able to recognize who the giants were. He chose *their* shoulders rather than those of mental pygmies on which to stand. There is a lesson for us here. Do we choose giants for our "support," our inspiration, our advisors, teachers? Or are we content with whoever might be around? Advertising would have this process subverted. We are told to purchase products because athletes or TV stars use them. Contrarily, I need to motivate myself to be certain, absolutely certain, because my real life *does* depend on it, that the women and men whose examples I follow, whose ideas are built on, are giants, nothing less. Otherwise, I will not be able to say, in summary of my life, "If I have seen further . . ." or "If I have been able to love, it is because I have followed the style of lovers before me."

PART 5
Eternal Questions

*For Kay and Walter Kromm
friends*

45
Questions without Answers

The wise person doesn't pray to be given the right answers. Rather, the woman or man of true wisdom seeks to learn the proper questions. Because answers change; the questions remain eternal. This does not mean that there are no everlasting truths. But it signifies that our understandings of these truths develop. One of the fundamental questions we ask is "Who am I?" The person who would answer that in precisely the same way at age forty-five as at twenty-five is spiritually dead. For some the answer to "Who am I?" may evolve almost daily. Of course, there is a danger here that we become so wishy-washy that our character is effected. But the issue here is not *that* aspect, irresponsible change. The point is growth through a kind of grace of questioning. Perhaps each of us will need to draw up our own set of important questions —those that will be most meaningful to us personally. The answers to some of these will depend on the answer to others. Take two closely related examples: What is the meaning of life? What is my purpose in relation to the meaning of life? As the response to the first changes, so will that to the second. What is my relationship with God? That can only be determined insofar as we react to a previous query: What is the nature of God? Surely anyone who is serious about faith encounters God differently as time passes. Surely, too, that results in a modified relationship with God. But this will be a development, rather than a regression, only when we are serious about the questions we ask. Wisdom is not the result of luck. Searching is a difficult human activity. Learning is a satisfying human experience. Perhaps each of us would benefit from establishing a list of the most important questions—the eternal questions. They'll have nothing to do with hairstyles, consumer products, social engagements, or the like. Instead, they will deal with the fundamentals of our being. Some of the questions may even be frightening initially: What is death? However in facing them we will learn—and lose—our fears and become more fully total persons.

46
Time, the Great Ally

The cliche has it that time is the enemy of man. Not so—time is one of our supreme assets. It is in time that we grow, we gain experience, we learn, we mature. To fail to comprehend this may be to live on a level of immature yearning. What a tragedy it would be to actually find the fountain of youth. Imagine being young for an entire lifetime! Youth can be a wonderful period in our lives, but it also is a preparatory period. All preparation with no goal is anticipation with no climax, windup with no pitch, practicing the scales with no concert performance. Time is fulfilling. Of course, this implies not only having experiences but being able to evaluate them as well. A woman or man who has just one meaningful experience in life has had a fuller existence than the person with hundreds of "events" that were lived through unanalyzed. Thus even a youth who can evaluate a single experience is more mature than an adult who has lived through all kinds of experiences that have made almost no impact on the individual. But how much more rewarding will be the life of that same youth, who has cultivated the habit of evaluating experiences, in maturity, when more experiences can be known in the light of the earlier known experiences. A forty-year-old who really wishes to be a twenty-year-old is in some important way probably a ten-year-old. Not in the sense of innocence but in the sense of ignorance. Each day fully lived guarantees that the next day will be even more fully lived. While the meaning of life is not bound up in an escape from our senses, it certainly cannot be found in an exclusive immersion in the senses. Wisdom is an attribute of true maturity and generally this maturity is arrived at through time, a time which is the great ally of human growth.

47
Tradition Is Not Convention

Before the Gospel there was the gospel. That's what tradition means to a Christian. Jesus Christ did not begin something totally new. His work was not a second creation *ex nihilo.* Rather he is a person who helped to fulfill the tradition of Israel. Christ brought a certain dimension that we Christians believe that tradition lacked. He continued that tradition, helped it to take almost a quantum leap. In doing this he implicitly recognized that this is a living tradition, not static, not inert, not backward looking. Thus tradition is to be very much opposed to convention with which it is sometimes confused. Some synonyms for *convention* include the following words: ordinary, commonplace, routine, stereotyped, inflexible, obstinate. Tradition is certainly not any of these. Tradition is vibrant, alive, informing, constantly developing. Convention deadens; it kills the spirit. Tradition gives life to the soul. And we, too, help tradition to be nourished. A living tradition not only maintains a continuity and identity with the past, it also must grow in each generation, as that generation gives its own input to tradition. Each generation *does* contribute one way or another. The following idea would be impossible but perhaps the thought is illuminating: For a generation not to contribute to tradition is in itself a negative way of contribution. The same is true of each of us as well. In our lives we participate in tradition to a positive or negative degree and if positive, to a more or less degree. To adopt Christ's own metaphor, tradition is a vine which grows toward the omega. We are the branches. Healthy, vital branches assist the overall vine in its growth. Sickly or dead branches hinder the completion. Tradition certainly does not mean change for its own sake. All change is not necessarily growth. The vine has a direction in which to proceed. Not all direction is upward.

48
Suffering

There are a number of distinctions to be made about suffering. One of these is the difference between my suffering and another's. I can accept my own, if I choose, can even see it as a gift from God. This can be a great virtue on my part. But it is immoral for me to accept another person's suffering in the same way. In fact, I must work for its eradication. Even when that other man or woman heroically accepts misfortune as a kind of visitation of grace, my efforts need to be aimed at eradicating suffering—a kind of evil. It isn't the actual pain that is good. Pain is not good, although the purification through pain can be good; so can the manner in which this suffering is accepted. But for me to look at another's grief and immobilize any possible relief resources I have because such suffering is good for the other person would be a significant failure on my part. Too often Christians smugly sit back when someone is being injured and think how lucky that person is because her or his reward will be great in heaven. That's a cop-out on a demonic scale. Albert Camus excoriated Christians on just this problem—being too next worldish and thus absolving ourselves from concentrating on solving the problems on this earth at this time. If Christ had had the same attitude, there would have been no Incarnation. His becoming flesh is proof that we must not flee from the world but rather involve ourselves with it in some holy way. Joseph Conrad's character in *Lord Jim* put it this way: "In the destructive element immerse yourself." Through such a process we can overcome. Ever since Saint Augustine's *City of God*, Christianity has coffered the notion that the world is evil and only heaven is good. This indeed seems to have discouraged many from participating in the affairs of earth. It seems to have kept people from helping to alleviate the sufferings of other people. This has made it easy for us to excuse ourselves from exerting ourselves on behalf of our neighbors' sufferings. And such a failure is, in fact, anti-Christian.

49
Our Crosses

Simon the Cyrene is a very special person in history. He alone literally picked up Christ's cross and carried it. According to scripture he didn't necessarily do it willingly, and there may be a tremendous symbol in that for all of us. Nevertheless, Simon carried the burden, and we can imagine the impact that had on the rest of Simon's life. And what about for us? Are we carrying the cross? How far, how long? In what spirit? Christianity is not a call to comfort. It is a call to communion with Jesus and his mission. Christ is asking us every moment to relieve his ache somewhat by bearing our share of the burden. How do we respond? He asks, we are told, when the least of his sisters and brothers ask us. There is nothing abstract or theoretical about this. Anybody in pain is Christ in pain. Anyone in need is Jesus suffering. Most of us can be very creative in our excuses as to why we don't do something on cross-carrying occasions. Too few of us accept the challenge that so often comes in the form of a plea, a moan, a hope which we, as Christians, must be prepared to hear—sometimes even if it is unsounded. People starve in a number of ways. Some because there is no food. Others because there is no love, no meaningful human contact. Some persons despair. Others grieve. Some feel themselves to be misfits. Others exaggerate their achievements because of a terrific need for a respect they feel they have not earned. And how do we work for them, love for them, help to lift their crosses—which are all parts of Christ's world cross? Many of us never do. Or occasionally, when we involve ourselves, it's from 7:00–9:00 on Monday evenings or in an otherwise begrudging fashion. Some people call that Christian charity. Others recognize the "minimal" attitude for what it is—a mere ploy to rid ourselves of guilt feelings which are well earned.

50
Lonely Is Not Alone

Lonely is not a synonym for *alone*. The word *lonely* connotes isolation and dejection, a missed absence of companions when it is applied to persons. The root of *alone*, however, is in two words: *all one*. This means the opposite of isolation and dejection. The emphasis is not on the *one* but on the *wholly* one. It means complete by oneself. How many of us can actually feel that way? It is not easy to be full in oneself, to respect oneself, and to self-develop to such a degree that a person looks forward to long periods of being alone. For some who enjoy this oneness, they realize that because of their relationship with Christ they are never lonely. They cultivate the chances to be alone so that they can actually savor the moments with God alone, the moments when their unity with the Creator can be both enjoyed and developed. This implies quite a special human being. Too often we are frantic for companionship—for the team or the club or the class or the party or the movie or the TV. Immersion in such activities will free us from having to face the basic issues of existence. Such trivial busyness will keep us from intimate contact with ourselves. The kingdom of heaven is within each of us, yet how seriously do we try to make contact with it? Not only is there no need to go "out there" in most instances, but rather it is spiritually harmful to look outside of ourselves while ignoring what is by nature within us. The woman or man who can be alone—can be *together* in the self—is the kind of person we can admire, can hold as a model. The quest for wholeness for individual unity is one of the great journeys a life can make, indeed should make. There is no easy route to being properly alone. But making the trip is learning to find what the meaning of life is.

51
Saints

We need heroes. They show us the wonders of life, the possibilities in life. They fill us with a sense of pride and gratitude in our own humanity. Life and love are communal. It is through community that we mature. So it is proper that we seek a community, a neighborhood, of people who inspire us to better living. Churches have realized that and have given us saints. However, these need to be supplemented with our own personal set of human champions—or champion humans—whose experiences are more particularly like our own. Saint Theresa of Lisieux was no doubt a great woman, but there is little in her life that parallels ours. Biographers tell us that from the age of about six she wanted to become a nun. God is said to have showered flower petals on her head. People trying to raise a family, earn a living, resist sexual temptations, or seriously work for better race relations or prison reform may think that Theresa's experiences were "nice" but they won't be able to connect with them. Saint Paul got knocked off a horse and blinded by God, even scolded by God. *Why wouldn't* Paul believe after an experience like that! It makes a neat contrast, of course, with Judas's contact with Christ. As an apostle, Judas, too, was called, and he gave a resounding no. Paul's yes is important, but the circumstances are outside our own life patterns. Nevertheless, heroes are necessary for our sense of humanity, of growth, of community in which we are spiritually nourished. If we fail to see the heroic in otherwise ordinary mortals, we may be in such a state of despair that it is dangerous to our own development. Are we so discouraged by political chicanery, by military lying, by ecclesiastical blundering, by friends letting us down that we finally believe that everybody has a price? Or can we find those human beacons that will guide us through the ordinariness of existence? One further note on this may also be put in the form of a rhetorical question: Do we have the confidence to lead our own lives so that we may be beacons for others?

52
The Sanctity of Words

Martyrs and other exemplary missionaries notwithstanding, Christianity has made almost no impact among North American Indian tribes. The reason may be that, as one observer has indicated, "Wherever the native had the opportunity to gain a deeper insight into the teachings of Christianity and to watch, at the same time, the white man's way of living, he very soon became fully aware of the painful discrepancy between theory and practice." Nowhere could this be plainer than in the lies that Christians told Indians. Broken agreements are now legend. Why has the Christian traditionally had so little regard for the true word? After all, it is part of the religious symbolism of our creed that the Word was made flesh. Yet the concept has had little significance for us. For the Indians, the word is sacred. To utter a word is to participate in the creative act.

In the Uitoto creation myth we find that "in the beginning, the word gave origin to the Father." Hence any further use of words borders on the sacred. Misuse, of course, is sacrilege. Silence, then, is frequently the only appropriate form of communication. Those who enjoy a deep love or friendship understand this. They don't need to make noise to prove their affection for each other. A lover's glance is often sufficient; a Hollywood cliche might spoil a moment. Yet words are used so carelessly by Christians who otherwise can be so scrupulous about counting first Friday masses attended, rosaries prayed, the number of sick visited. The most obscene use of words is in advertising. What does the word *great* mean, for a simple example? Is Mary, the Mother of Jesus, great? Is a Buick car great? Are they both somehow great in the same way? Do we freely endorse products for money? What would we say about cigarettes or liquor, say, for a $5,000 fee? Are we conscious that we cheapen words, those primary tools by which women and men can communicate with each other and leave a permanent record of their very passage through this earth? Are words holy for us?

53
Freedom

Time may be thought of as the duration in which we achieve our freedom as creatures of God. There are, of course, many definitions of the concept of time, but the one indicated here is suggested as a concept for committed Christians. The emphasis is on two words: *achieve* and *freedom*. Our personal time is that period of history in which we live, in which we either work for the advancement of humanity or fail to do so, in which we use the freedom we have (each of us in varying degrees) or neglect it. Freedom for the committed Christian—and that phrase is redundant—can be seen as the obligation we have to do good. How well we fulfill that obligation will partly depend on whether or not we even recognize it as a duty. If freedom is seen only in negative terms, for example, in lack of restraints or personal hindrances, we won't get very far along the route of spiritual progress. If the idea of freedom is bound up with the notion of pleasure, then, too, we stymie ourselves. Freedom for the believer is the gift to choose between cooperating with the adventure of human existence or not cooperating (by either indifference or hostility). If the world has meaning, we must learn what it is and direct our lives accordingly. If we fail to do so, we fail to be fully human. We are *free* to do so, but we will imprison ourselves in the hell of human failure. The only real achievement is along the lines here implied—on the magnitude of human advancement. Our achievements will only be small compared to the kinds of spectacular results we think we would like to attain, but they will be real. A drop of love can purify an ocean of despair. An atom of passion can move a mountain of indifference. A second of pure attention to God can make up for an eon of neglect. In the time given us on earth, we can achieve all of these freedoms. We can choose to be with humanity or against it, with God or against God. That, in the ultimate analysis, is the most overwhelming freedom imaginable—and perhaps the only one with which to really be concerned.

54
Luxuries

Not everyone feels the same way about luxuries. Some of us see them as badges of success, of having made it. Others see luxuries as reward for hard work, something we deserve by nature of our application to industry. Another segment of humanity is indifferent to luxuries. If they have them, they are taken in stride; if they do not have them, there are no complaints. And another group despises luxury and all it stands for. In their minds, luxuries get in the way of living. They feel the danger of getting caught up in the race for acquiring. Then there is the attention necessary to protecting what we have, when we do acquire. All of this energy, this last set of people believes, deflects our attention from what is really important in human existence. It is undoubtedly worthwhile, spiritually, for each of us to reevaluate our attitudes toward luxuries which really are the result of a state of mind. In terms of material things, for example, a second car, a power saw, a television set, or a certain style of dishes may be a necessity to some, a luxury to others. Our mind set toward objects is, in large measure, what determines their status in this way. In reality it seems that we generally do not give much thought to the items we gather about us over the years, items that may have the effect of weighing our spirits down as we inevitably become attached to them. Let me think for a moment of all of the knickknacks, clothes, trinkets, and even bulkier things that I have gathered and that either come close to overwhelming me or that insidiously distract me from the true Christian spirit. Not only must I be careful not to fall into the trap of acquisitiveness, I must also be cautious about helping to ensnare someone else: my children, for example. Luxuries to them may be nothing more than the burden of my own questionable habits. This burden I inflict on them through some false sense of vicarious pride —see, they share *my* values! What a shame. And what a tragedy. I risk corrupting the very people who are closest to me in all the world.

55
On Being Perfect

In Scripture, Christ has commanded that we be perfect even as the Father is in heaven. Surely Jesus is not asking the impossible. We cannot be without flaw—human nature implies imperfection. What then could he have meant? Surely it is not in achieving some absolutely perfect condition that we are saved. If that were true, who would be saved? We only have to look at the saints to realize that *perfection is not the requirement:* Saint Catherine of Siena clearly had an obnoxious personality at times. Joan of Arc attempted suicide. As a father, Gandi was a remarkable failure. And so on, as for each of us and each of them. Yet they are nevertheless saints—and so we, too, can become nevertheless among the "saved," not by attaining sanctity, whatever that means, but by striving to attain it. The whole is clearly greater than the mere sum of its parts: Salvation is a wholeness that is far greater than the sum of each of our individual acts toward it. That can be very comforting, and it should be. So often we are easily discouraged in our efforts because of many small and occasional major failures. Persistence sometimes takes a beating. Nevertheless a stick-to-itiveness in the face of this human condition is what can be heroic in our lives. The term we hear so often, *heroic sanctity,* is, in fact, redundant. All sanctity implies is a tough grinding out under commonplace conditions, an approach to the ordinary which is extraordinary. It is when the spotlight is *not* on them that stars are actually made. Football heroes don't just happen to perform well on Saturday afternoons; they worked a great deal during the week in preparation. Not that the saved expect to be in the limelight. It is in attention to the small that the large is achieved. And within this framework, it is in constantly returning our attention to the small, on the very many occasions that we are distracted, that our own personal fulfillment depends. And that's what sanctity is: wholeness, fulfillment.

56
Two Kinds of Knowledge

There has long been a distinction made between two types of knowledge. There is the knowledge of things created, and this exerts a proper attraction on most of us. There is, more importantly, self-knowledge which, unfortunately, does not attract us nearly as much. Knowledge of that which is outside ourselves is very important and becomes a problem only when we make that the goal of our journey in life. It complements, in a very important way, self-knowledge but must be held in balance so as not to crowd out our search for the true interior of our beings. For it is deep within ourselves that the meaning of the universe is to be found. Very few persons throughout history seem to have learned the full value of this truth. Socrates is honored for having taught his pupils to *know thyself*, but he has not been honored with observance by most of humanity. So much of an emphasis is being placed on community, on social movements, on helping others in a relatively non-ordered way that such activity is used as an excuse to mask a significant observation: that it is too difficult for most of us to attempt to search ourselves for the meaning of the universe. The message the mystics have for us is that while there is indeed a very real world "out there," there is a more real world within each of us. What the meaning of this cosmic center is, each must learn, individually. I am the living text for me and the only text. I cannot learn the lesson from what another has experienced or has written. Some can help me on the periphery, but the heart of the matter is in the heart of my soul. To ignore the truth from the Messenger is to put ourselves outside of that *community of individuals* who are the true seekers, who are willing to wrestle and struggle with the difficulties that self-knowledge implies to gain the freedom and light that self-knowledge promises.

57
Children and History

Having children is a way of communicating with history. A parent may simply go through the motions of generating a certain number of babies with no informing attitude in the process. But a more responsible father or mother will be creative in parenthood, will raise the children in a manner that reflects a certain awareness of history, of the direction in which the world is going. Currently some sociologists and psychologists are lamenting the absence of grandparents from a home environment as children grow. Part of the reason for this concern is because a historical dimension within the family itself has been taken from young boys and girls. But now there is another problem on the vista, one which arises because couples are refusing to have children—have almost a contempt for families. What is going to happen to couples who grow old, reach the age of grandparenthood, but have no grandchildren? They will never known the love of children nor will they thus have the spiritual benefits of grandchildren. Clearly everyone does not have to be a parent to be fulfilled. To say otherwise is to be ignorant of numerous saints, scholars, and otherwise whole personalities. Nevertheless the normal route through which most of us mature is through family love. Size of family is not implied here; quality of family life is. The parent who accepts responsibility is not a spectator of history but a participant. This mother or father will have an idea, a goal, toward which the child will be initially guided. This goal will be so important—it is, after all, the meaning of life—that all else will be geared to it. Here, then, is one level of dialogue with history. It really is a matter of not being indifferent, of not letting events work their will on us, but of participating in them because life has a meaning. Those who cannot communicate with history, be it through committed celibacy, cared-for children, or some other fulfillment, are handicapped.

58
Reincarnation

There is a significant number of people on this earth who profess religious beliefs that include the idea of reincarnation. Even for those who do not hold this belief it is interesting to speculate on our own personal futures *as if* we were certain of reincarnation. If we truly thought that we would come back again, in a form of life which we "earned" or "deserved" (based on how we conducted ourselves in this term in the world), would we behave any differently than we now do? It's a question that we can readily put to militarists, technologists, educators, advertisers, artists, writers, theologians, anarchists, conservatives, liberals . . . Is the world I am preparing one in which I wish to live? Do certain advertisers actually want to participate in the world that they are helping to shape? What of the kinds of values certain teachers are inculcating into our students—would these faculty members really wish to be forced to live them out two generations from now? The peddlars of television mediocrity use this excuse: We are giving the public what it wants. Do those peddlars want to be reincarnated into the kind of world they are assisting in establishing? There would be a kind of justice in the simplified reincarnation described here—a poetic justice which might give satisfaction to some observers. Yet if we lived our lives from the point of view suggested here, we might be more thoughtful in our attitudes and in our acts. Our children and our grandchildren, in one way of thinking, are a kind of incarnation of ourselves. To all Christians, every person, including the not yet born, is to be seen as Christ. What kind of a world are we preparing for Jesus, for each Jesus in the world? How are we carrying forward the work of other Christs before us? How are we making a world for the *becoming* Christs? From such a point of view, there really is no need to think of reincarnation, then, as far as the effects of our work goes. We need only put our work to the service of Christ.

59
Theologians All

Theologians have long been an important group of the members of the Christian community. However, there may be some misunderstanding regarding who they are. This is particularly true in our era when people can get university degrees in theology and are thus generally looked on as theologians. But a true theologian is not to be judged by the amount of subject matter mastered. Rather, a theologian in the fullest sense is a man or woman in whom God is prayerfully present. Scholarship is not absent from this person's experience; it is, however, embraced in a contemplative tradition—part of the Christian meditative historical process that gives theological knowledge its special illumination. The holy woman or man, ignorant of theological schools and trends, is far more worthy to be considered a theologian than is a person with various college degrees, who "knows" the field but leads a life which is not virtuous. Just as a politician may not necessarily be the best American, nor a wealthy man a good man, nor a beautiful woman a kind one, nor a well-read person a good teacher, nor a strong man a courageous one, neither is every one who is called a theologian actually a true one. Perhaps we might consider that each of us is called, in a certain way, to be more a theologian than we had at first suspected. Knowledge of theological matters is a good something for which we may profitably strive as Christians. But this knowledge must be planted in the soil of the contemplative awareness of Christ in our lives if it is to be rooted so that it might develop within us. The combination, then, of the awareness of the mystery of God in us and the wisdom stemming from the union of this experience with what has been called the science of God, is a combination that could lead us to the fuller life for which we search. We need not feel that true theologians are those *other* people. Each of us is able to be a theologian by virtue of a mature love of God in union with the intellectual search.